Presents

I CAN FLY

The Inspiring Story of the Zip Zap Children's Circus

©2019 Dr Zizz
ISBN: 978-0-620-83064-5
First published by Zip Zap 2019
More at drzizz.com

Printed by:
Tandym Print
Viking Way, Epping, Cape Town, 7475
Layout, colourising of illustrations, typesetting and design by Chip Snaddon: chipsnaddon.portfoliobox.net

Dr Zizz: *For my son. And for Shorty, who never grew up.*

Ayanda Nombelwu: *I would like to thank my dad Hugo Valicenti for supporting me through the whole drawing process.*

Special thanks to the following Catchers who dared to dream with us to make this book a reality:

Roelof Botha

syllk39

Dr Christa Weyers and her team at Optima@RustenVrede hospital, one of the first in-patient settings in South Africa

where children with emotional problems can be admitted with a parent for a therapeutic programme:

www.optima@rustenvrede.com

Like me,

this story starts small.

One man called Brent.
One circus tent.

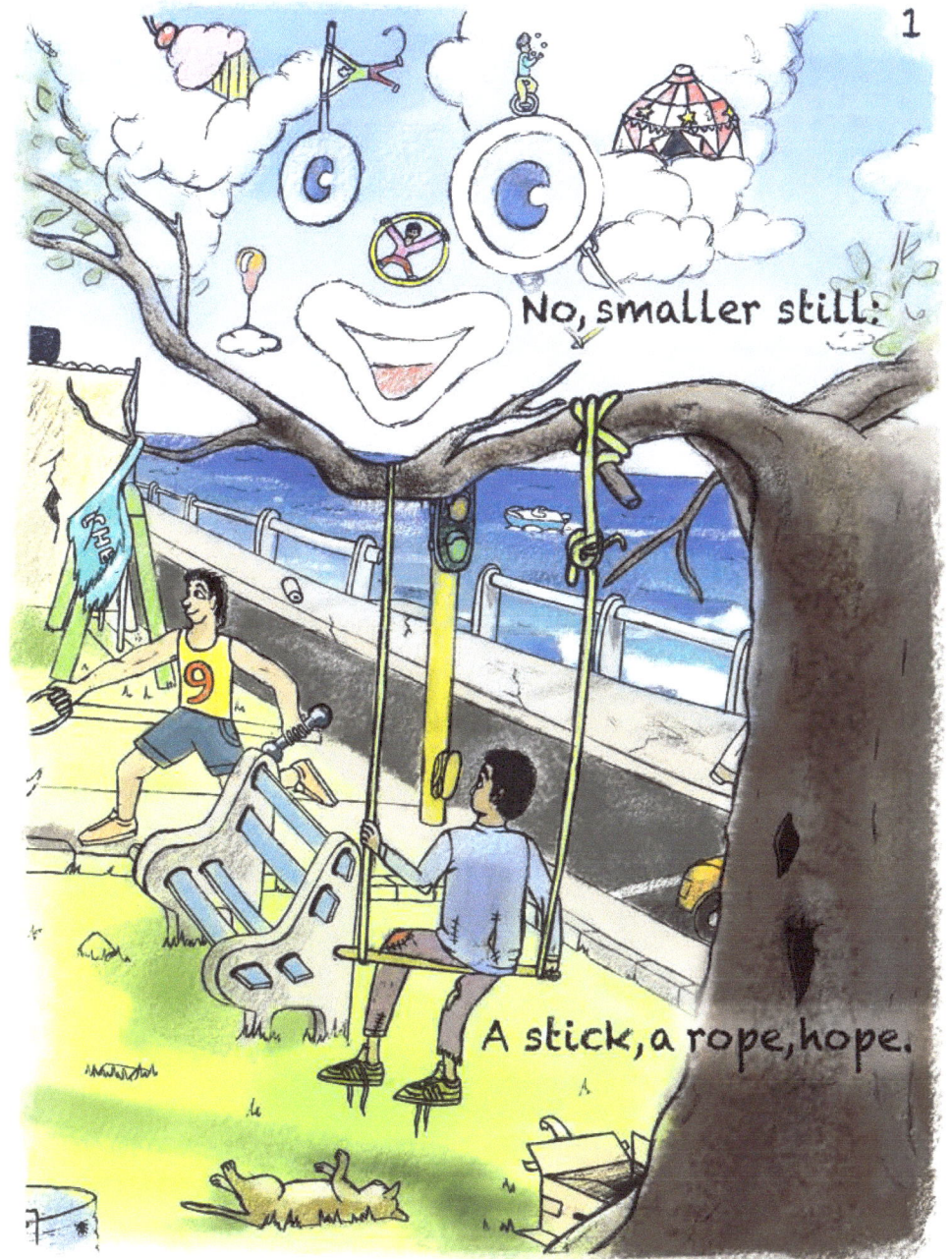

No, smaller still.

A stick, a rope, hope.

I'm Lucky Mtuff
and I'm sleeping rough
in a tin can far beneath the stars.

Lucky me, Lucky me!

At night I can see
Venus, Jupiter and Mars.

And this dog is Luna Lee.

She shares her food and bed
with me.

One day the circus came to town.
Or rather, one man did:

Just Brent, no tent.

COME ★ TRY
OUR ★ KIND ★
★ OF ★ FLYING
5rand ★

Lucky doesn't have five bob. He doesn't have a job.

He watched that show through bars.

He couldn't see the stars.

But in his head a small voice said:

Just believe
and don't let go

and you will join
this circus show!

"WAIT," I said, "STOP!
I'm Lucky Mtuff
and you need me!" I said.
"And I need a bed."

Said Brent, "I don't have a cent.
My troupe's just too small
—and you're not tall.

My catcher's gone, my clown's left town—

this Star lord's down!"

"Please! I'll go where you go...
We can be... a children's show!"

But Brent said no.
"All shows are for children," he said.

I was desperate. I was under-fed.
I yelled, "Wait a minute!
I mean a show with **children in it.**
Grown-ups run away from the circus, not to it.

They're afraid they won't know how to do it."

"And your dog?"

Brent looked at Luna Lee, then me.
"This is a circus, not a zoo."

"She's my friend," I said.
"The dog comes too."

And so I learned the rules of Circus School:

1. Chop wood.

2. Carry water (or poles and sticks).

3. Practice tricks.

4. Paint the walls.

5. Rig the lights.

6. Wash Brent's tights!

"Okay," said Brent with a frown, "I need a clown.

And we need a name for our game.

Something catchy and cute."

He pulled out a moth-eaten ringmaster's suit.

"We can be *Lentil and Brecky* – or *Brecky and Lent*?"

We settled on *Iron Bru and Leena Loo.*

We aimed for fame, and fortune too.

And you know what?
I was funny.
We did some shows, and we made money.

But in my head a small voice said:

Who dares grins,

Who tries wins!

If you dream

It will come true

And you can be a FLYER too!

"No," said Brent, "you're much too small.
I'm **** scared that you will fall.
And I can't catch you, I'm a flyer—
sure, if a catcher can catch you, then a catcher can
but I'm not that lucky catching man."

"Brent," I said, "if I fall I will stand up,
look the audience in the eye,
and do it again.
And if I die flying

then I was Lucky to live,

Lucky to try,

Lucky to fly.

Now raise your bar.
I know I am a superstar."

Brent went quiet. Then he gave me a very short book.

I took a quick look.

HOW TO STAY ALIVE:

"Believe," it said, "and you will fly.
Just leave the earth, and touch the sky.
When someone's your friend,
he won't let go.

When someone's your friend

it's more than just a show."

I closed one eye.

Then Lucky flew...

(And Luna Lee did too.)

Who says you can't teach an old dog new tricks?

Now Lucky's surrounded by stars.
One more diamond in the sky,
one white diamond on his eye.

All because the child was father to the man
and said to him:

"I think I can."

This is me today.

I'm Lucky Mtuff
and life is still rough.

But now I am... BUFF!

We have a school, we have a tent.

And we have Brent.

He's the **Zip**, and we're the **Zap**!

He's the best friend that we've ever had.

"Can this whole circus call you **DAD**?"

24

This is not a tall story.
Though it's short, it's true.
It shows you what a child can do.
So remember that – 'cause you're a child,
you're Lucky too:

The sky is love
and it's the limit
when you put
your whole heart in it.

CAPAB DRAMA & ZIP ZAP CIRCUS presents:

TRICK!
who dares grins . . .

director: Jana van Niekerk
circus acts: Brent van Rensburg
designs: Keith Anderson
lighting: Malcolm Hurrell

8 dec 1996 – 5 Jan 1997
under the Big Top
in the Founder's Gardens
AT THE NICO

Everybody's different...

...colour the picture in your way!

www.ingramcontent.com/pod-product-compliance
Lightning Source LLC
Chambersburg PA
CBHW060911270326

41933CB00005B/211